Looking After People with Late HIV Disease

by
Jan Welch and Jenny Newbury

The Patten Press in association with The Lisa Sainsbury Foundation

ISBN 1 872229 2 55

Prepared and typeset at The Patten Press, The Old Post Office, Newmill, Penzance, Cornwall TR20 4XN
Printed and bound in Great Britain by Billing and Sons Limited, Worcester.

Contents

Foreword, Dr. Andrew Hoy vii

Preface viii

Acknowledgements ix

1 Preparation for illness, 1

2 Terminal Care for people with AIDS - general principles, 5

3 Common distressing symptoms and treatment, 13

4 Hospital-based care, 39

5 Care in the community, 46

6 Hospice care, 51

7 Deaths and funerals, 54

8 Care of the bereaved, 56

9 Care for the carers, 58

Further reading and reference, 60
Useful addresses, 61

Foreword

As the AIDS epidemic progresses, so the realisation grows that we as a society and as professionals do not yet have many of the answers to halt this new and devastating disease. It is also unlikely that the mortality will reduce in the near future, in spite of intensive efforts to understand the pathology and develop new techniques of prevention, immunisation and treatment. We all therefore need to learn how best to care for people entering the terminal phase of HIV infection.

Over the past generation, the United Kingdom has been at the forefront of the evolution of the "Hospice Movement". This philosophy of palliative care has found support in many other countries of the world, especially the United States of America and Canada. Although hospice principles are most easily employed in caring for people with relatively predictable terminal illness such as cancer, these same principles have been adapted and applied for the care of patients with non-malignant fatal illness. End-stage HIV infection unfortunately fits this description at present.

Perhaps the kernel of hospice philosophy is the notion of patient-centred and directed care. Such ideas serve to underline the crucial importance of symptom control, psycho-social support, counselling, confidentiality, mobilisation and coordination of all available resources.

There are undoubted differences between the average hospice patient and a person dying of AIDS, however there are far more problems in common, with similar solutions. The new breed of health care professionals concerned with people dying from AIDS needs to learn as much as they can about hospice philosophy, just as all those working in palliative care need to re-examine their assumptions and working practices in the light of the advent of AIDS. This will almost certainly include the readiness and skill to offer care to dying AIDS patients.

This timely book serves to demonstrate that we must all be part of the modern "Hospice Movement".

Andrew Hoy
Medical Director
The Princess Alice Hospice
Esher, Surrey

Preface

AIDS is no longer a disease mainly confined to the large London centres, where most of the early cases were seen. Cases of AIDS have now been reported throughout the United Kingdom, and some of those patients who moved to London for treatment later wish to return home to die. As a result many more health care professionals are becoming involved with the care of people with AIDS.

At present most AIDS cases in the United Kingdom have acquired their infection by homosexual contact. These men are often particularly articulate and informed. Like many other patients, they wish to retain control over their lives and deaths, and to this end they have developed sophisticated organisations for support and for sharing information. They often have strong views about their investigations and treatment, particularly if they have already seen friends become ill and die from AIDS, and commonly request new - and as yet unproven - drugs.

Most homosexual men altered their behaviour once the transmission of HIV infection became understood. Although we are still likely to see many cases of AIDS in gay men who have been infected before this, and there is evidence that risky sexual practices are again becoming more common, it seems likely that in the future an increasing proportion of AIDS patients will have acquired their infection by other routes such as intravenous drug use and heterosexual contact. This means that more women are likely to contract HIV, and as, the infection is readily transmitted vertically in human reproduction, paediatric infection will also increase. In some countries heterosexual transmission has always been the major route of spread, and HIV infection is a common problem in immigrant families from central Africa. Infection by the use of infected blood, blood products or organ transplants is now extremely rare in countries which have facilities for screening and heat treatment, but there remain some patients infected before this who have yet to develop AIDS.

There is now an enormous amount of literature on AIDS, and many excellent books have been written which cover pathogenesis, epidemiology, counselling, infection control, the treatment of opportunistic infections and tumours, and antiviral agents. This book does not aim specifically to cover these topics, but instead to concentrate on the management of the patient who is dying from AIDS. It is addressed to any health care professional who needs a practical manual on how this can best be organised, on symptom control, and on the particular problems encountered by some patients who have acquired infection by the various routes outlined above.

NB In the text, for convenience of expression, patients have been referred to as 'he' and nurses as 'she'.

Acknowledgements

The authors would like to thank the many people who have helped in the preparation of this book, and in particular Dr. Caroline Bradbeer, Dr. David Barlow and Dr. Bill O'Neill of St. Thomas' Hospital, Dr. Veronica Moss of the Mildmay Mission Hospital and Miss Vera Darling of the Lisa Sainsbury Foundation.

Chapter 1

PREPARATION FOR ILLNESS

Individuals who know that they are infected by the human immunodeficiency virus (HIV) are generally very aware that their lifespan is likely to be reduced. Often they have seen friends dying from AIDS, and so have first-hand experience of many of the problems. Symptomatic patients are particularly likely to worry about the future, as they can see that they are already being affected by HIV and feel that the development of AIDS is inevitable, and that death will follow soon afterwards. It is worth pointing out that the definition of AIDS is an arbitrary one encompassing a variety of conditions, many of which are compatible with an excellent quality of life for several years. Some of the most frightened patients are those with non-specific but debilitating symptoms, such as tiredness and night sweats, who find the uncertainty of waiting to develop AIDS very difficult to cope with. Once the diagnosis of AIDS has been made they may even find it easier to come to terms with their

mortality, and paradoxically then make much more of their lives.

Coming to terms with mortality

Most of these people appreciate the opportunity for discussion of their health and the future, and unnecessary fears can often be allayed by this. It is helpful to talk over aspects of terminal care whilst the patients are well, as this also enables them to contribute views about their future management at a time when rational decisions are easier to make. They should also be encouraged to put their affairs in order. Once this has been done, and the worst has been faced and dealt with, many people find it easier to be more positive about the remainder of their lives. This confidence can enable them to enjoy new interests and activities. Patients frequently become involved in the many organisations that have been developed by and for people with AIDS. Some people perhaps become over-involved, and can then find that AIDS has become their major reasons for living, rather than for dying. This can result in 'burn-out' and depression, particularly when many friends and colleagues are ill or dying from AIDS. Participation in activities outside this area may help people with AIDS to retain a sense of perspective.

Determining the patient's wishes

Discussion about the future is easily started by the patient and doctor together making a written record of the former's arrangements and wishes, by filling in a form outlining the information needed (see example). This is then kept in the notes, and a photocopy can be given to other professionals concerned with the patient's care, for example on admission to hospital or transfer to a hospice. This improves continuity of management, particularly when out-patient/in-patient care is shared between different medical teams. Patients are often relieved to have had an opportunity to talk about arrangements, and are pleased to have their wishes recorded. The date should be noted on the form, because following discussion, patients often take appropriate action, such as making a will. The form can then be updated. The discussion may also identify problem areas which need specific counselling, for example, with a re-

lationship. The identification then provides the professional with an indication of how and to whom the patient should be further referred.

Informing friends and family

Obtaining details about both the legal next of kin, for example the patient's father, and a nominated next of kin provides an opportunity for discussion of relationships with family and close friends. Asking about a nominated next of kin allows for recognition of the importance of a lover or close friend. Generally the nominated next of kin is fully aware of the patient's diagnosis from the beginning, but family are often not told the truth until the patient has AIDS. The wish to tell at this stage may be precipitated by repeated admission to hospital, or by marked changes in appearance.

Many people wish to shield one or more members of their family from their diagnosis of AIDS. This can result in great strain for the patient, who may have to dissimulate and conceal medication, and probably also for the family, who frequently suspect the diagnosis. Obviously the patient is the only one who can decide whom should be told, but it is worth encouraging him or her to look at the situation from the relation's point of view. A mother, for example, who knows that her son may only have a few months to live will have the opportunity of supporting him during this period, and have some time to come to terms with his death. This will not be the case if her son dies unexpectedly, and she may then find his death even harder to bear.

Confidentiality

It is important to record who knows what, so that confidentiality is not broken. This also applies to the patient's GP. Asymtomatic patients with HIV may not wish their GP to know, although when they are unwell they are usually happier for information about them to be passed on.

The Department of Social Security and other organisations such as housing departments often require medical certificates and letters. It is obviously essential to obtain and record the patient's consent before divulging information to these bodies. In some cases the patients may prefer to avoid mention of AIDS, and the practitioner may use and note more discreet terms, for example 'skin cancer'. Where there are major housing problems, however, the diagnosis of AIDS is often helpful in expediting rehousing.

Religion

It is useful to establish and record whether the patient has any religious convictions. If so, it may be appropriate to establish links with, for example, a hospital chaplain or a local priest.

Making a will

The subject of making a will is an important one to discuss, and any action taken should be recorded. It is worth stressing to patients how difficult their dying intestate can be for their family and friends. Obviously it is much easier for someone to write their will whilst well than it is in the middle of the night in hospital with pneumonia; making a will when unwell is also likely to add to the anxiety of the illness. Many individuals feel that they have nothing to leave, but when their assets are discussed in more detail there are often many personal possessions which they would like to be given to certain people. It is useful if the unit has links with a sympathetic solicitor who can help.

Resuscitation and terminal care

In some circumstances it may be appropriate to ventilate a patient with respiratory failure due to AIDS. Patients' views are naturally coloured by experiences of friends dying from AIDS, but most patients agree that they would like to be resuscitated if they are likely to return to an active life afterwards. A discussion on this topic often leads to consideration of other aspects of dying, and gives patients the opportunity to express fears and to record their views on the extent of investigations and treatment they would like towards the end.

3

Example of Front Sheet for file

Clinic Name _____

Patient's name _____

Date (Please date any changes)

NEXT OF KIN
Name
Address
Tel
State of knowledge

NOMINATED NEXT OF KIN
Name
Address
Tel
State of knowledge

GENERAL PRACTITIONER
Name
Address
Tel
State of knowledge
Permission to write YES/NO

DSS
State of knowledge

RELIGION

WILL
Discussed YES/NO
Written YES/NO

RESUSCITATION
Discussed YES/NO
Conclusion

Chapter 2

TERMINAL CARE FOR PEOPLE WITH AIDS - general principles

The diagnosis of AIDS indicates severe immunodeficiency, and is made by finding a major opportunistic infection or one of certain types of neoplasm. Most people with AIDS who recover from their first opportunistic infection - and this is now the great majority - can expect to return to relatively normal health, and work, for a year or more. Prophylaxis against infections, and the anti-retroviral drug zidovudine, prolong this period, the duration of which should increase further in the future as better anti-viral agents become available.

There then follows a slow decline when most patients develop intercurrent infections, often multiple, with increasing frequency. Some of these, such as perianal herpes and oral candidosis, can cause great discomfort. The most troublesome symptom at this stage is usually profound fatigue, and this may severely limit activities and make work impossible.

Malabsorption causing weight loss is universal, and patients often appear to age prematurely. Changes in appearance can also result from Kaposi's sarcoma, which often affects the face (especially the end of the nose), skin infections such as molluscum contagiosum, and side-effects of radiotherapy and chemotherapy, such as hair loss. All these changes require great adjustments for patients, as they come to terms with altered body image, reduced companionship and self-respect resulting from stopping work, less money, dependence on regular hospital attendances, and perhaps also the need to move to more suitable accommodation. Despite all their problems many of these people persist in fighting their illness, and wish to continue with uncomfortable investigations and treatments in the hope of prolonging their lives.

5

Recognising the terminal phase of illness

Eventually the patient may feel that enough has been done and he only wishes to be made comfortable. The doctor can help with this process by explaining the options available for diagnosis and treatment, and how likely each is to be helpful. As the patient becomes less well it will become increasingly inappropriate to search for covert causes of, say, pyrexia, whereas it will always be important to identify treatable causes of oral or perianal soreness. If the patient is confused, but has previously nominated someone to help make such decisions on his behalf, then discussion with this individual may obviously be helpful at this stage.

People with AIDS are often young, fit individuals who have never been seriously ill before, and fight their illness. Sometimes they make miraculous recoveries from seemingly moribund states. Consequently determining whether someone has reached the terminal stage of his illness can be extremely difficult, as may acceptance of this state by the patient. It is particularly difficult to assess a patient whose first presentation is with a severe opportunistic infection, perhaps because he has been too frightened to consider the possibility of AIDS and has delayed seeking medical attention.

It may also be difficult to recognise the terminal phase in the context of a long-standing relationship between doctor or nurse and patient. Because people with AIDS have so many problems, need a great deal of nursing and medical care, and are often of similar ages and outlook to their carers, close relationships inevitably develop. As this can make objectivity difficult, regular discussions with other health care workers about certain patients may help to clarify prognosis and determine likely future needs.

What sort of care does the patient need?

In the management of people with AIDS there is often no clear division between 'curative' and 'palliative' care. Much will often depend on the patient concerned and his current symptoms, and may change suddenly. At present AIDS is a terminal disease, and so it is important at all stages to consider the implications of drastic measures, such as intensive chemotherapy for widespread lymphoma, which may cause many side effects for little gain in life expectation. This must be balanced against the danger of making patients feel abandoned by witholding active treatment.

Most patients have firm ideas about the type and degree of care that they would like, and can be enabled to make major decisions about management. This may change during the course of the disease, however, and it needs to be remembered that someone who has all along wished to determine his treatment may suddenly prefer to shed this responsibility, temporarily or permanently.

As with other illnesses, many people with AIDS feel that natural remedies are beneficial in combating their disease. Complementary therapies are particularly popular with people who feel let down by the failure of conventional medicine to find a cure for them. A wide range of such treatments are available, ranging from relaxation techniques to acupuncture and homeopathy, and many patients derive great benefit from them. Occasionally, however, harm can result, as when patients are encouraged to stop conventional antibiotics used as prophylaxis against opportunistic infections, or are given substances such as germanium which have no proven benefit but can be toxic.

During the last stages of illness, the quality of life must be of paramount concern. Medical and nursing care should focus on minimising distressing symptoms, enabling patients to concentrate on enjoying what they can do. There is often a final period of semiconsciousness for a week or longer; excellent nursing care is vital in making a dignified and comfortable death possible.

Prophylaxis in terminal care

As opportunistic infections are so common in AIDS many patients are given drugs to prevent new or recurrent infections. Several types of tablets may be given for prophylaxis, and as patients often need other medication as well, drug interactions and side-effects can result. In the dying patient it is often desirable to rationalise treatment, but it may be difficult to know what to stop. In general at this stage it is most important to prevent problems which cause pain or distress, such as oral candidosis or perianal herpes, particularly as these can often develop rapidly after stopping prophylaxis. It is also desirable to prevent infections which threaten the quality of life, such as cytomegalovirus causing blindness, or toxoplasmosis causing fits, and so drugs against these should be continued as long as the patient can tolerate them.

Lifestyle and diet

Many people who discover that they have AIDS find that, after an initial period of grieving, they can reassess their priorities. Sometimes they can achieve more in these last years than they have ever done before. Trained counsellors can help patients come to terms with their illness. Doctors and nurses can also help by giving day-to-day support, and enabling patients to enjoy life as much as possible, for example by arranging medical back-up abroad so that a special holiday can be taken.

Ensuring that people with HIV infection are well nourished is an important part of management, as poor nutrition may decrease life expectation and increase morbidity. Antibody-positive people are generally keen to live as healthy a life as possible, and choose healthy foods such as fruit, vegetables and fish. Such a diet is likely to be low in calories, and this can contribute to weight loss. Consequently even well patients can benefit from a general discussion about their diet, and often find that if necessary they can increase caloric intake by the addition of high calorie drinks or snacks between meals. They may be reassured that, as long as they eat a variety of foods, they are likely to achieve an adequate intake of essential nutrients, and so there is no need to be over zealous about their choice of diet. They can also be advised that there is no need to be concerned about the effects of eating food high in saturated fats and cholesterol, as their primary needs are to maintain weight and nutritional status rather than to avoid heart disease.

As patients become more unwell problems such as anorexia, nausea and vomiting, mouth soreness, diarrhoea and malabsorption are associated with malnutrition and weight loss. Expert dietary advice can be of great benefit not only in improving nutritional status, but also in alleviating symptoms. When someone reaches the late stages of disease the goals may need to change: patients should be encouraged just to take what they want rather than feeling guilty about their poor intake.

If a patient is eating poorly because of lack of money then advice on eating well on a low income will be useful. Prescribable supplements such as 'Ensure', 'Fresubin' or 'Fortisip' may also help. These are available in a variety of flavours, both sweet and savoury, and so it may be worth trying several different types to find which is best tolerated. Most are sweet, and so are best tolerated by those who like sweet things, but many people find that these pall after a while. Free meals are available at some 'drop-in' centres, and by delivery services such as 'Meals-on-Wheels', and equipment such as a liquidiser or microwave may be provided by one of the charitable organisations.

Despite their healthy aims, many patients have unhealthy habits such as smoking and using sun-beds. As damage from these is likely to be in the distant future it seems unkind to attempt dissuasion. Patients who suffer from chronic fatigue may need to alter their daily routine by going to bed earlier, resting before going out for an evening, and rationing strenuous activities.

Symptom control

AIDS patients seem much less likely to have severe pain than those with solid tumours, but instead suffer from a variety of distressing symptoms such as oral soreness, perianal discomfort, nausea, and diarrhoea. Treatment of these specific symptoms is therefore generally more important than analgesia alone. In the terminal stages localised or generalised pain becomes more common and opioid analgesics are invaluable in allowing the patient a comfortable and dignified death.

Opioids

Opioids are also extremely helpful in giving symptomatic relief to patients with persistent, severe diarrhoea, and so may be indicated earlier in patients with this symptom than would otherwise be the case. In patients with diarrhoea a liquid preparation is often better absorbed than a tablet, and so is the ideal initial treatment, e.g. morphine elixir, given 4-hourly. Once the diarrhoea is controlled, tablets are more likely to be effective, and so the patient can continue on the same daily dose of morphine, but take it in the form of slow release tablets.

If a patient needs morphine for analgesia it is generally easiest to start with morphine elixir, as the dose can be titrated every 4 hours until the pain is controlled. When this has been achieved, slow release morphine can be substituted as above. If the taste of morphine elixir is disliked, diamorphine tablets can be substituted, but this is a much less flexible method as only 10 mg. tablets are available. If the patient cannot take oral medication, good control of pain or diarrhoea can be achieved by the use of a syringe driver (see below).

Patients who misuse drugs may need high does of opioids to control pain. These can be administered easily in hospital, but special arrangements must be made for out-patients, who are likely to need a daily prescription to prevent drug misuse.

The most common side-effects of opioids are constipation, sedation and nausea. Nausea is usually transient, resolving after a couple of weeks. An antiemetic should be prescribed initially, although most patients will not need to use it. If sleep is poor, a single small dose of haloperidol at night is effective sedation and will also reduce day-time nausea. Tolerance to the effects of opioids on the bowel does not develop, and so, unless the patient has diarrhoea, prophylaxis against constipation should be given. Regular oral lactulose is an effective treatment for patients who can tolerate liquids. If swallowing is impossible regular suppositories or enemas may be necessary.

Psychotropic drugs

People with AIDS are often highly sensitive to the effects of drugs on the central nervous system, and so a small dose should be given initially. Antipsychotic drugs such as chlorpromazine and haloperidol are useful in controlling anxiety and restlessness in the terminal stages, and also act as anti-emetics. Benzodiazepines such as diazepam are helpful if large components of anxiety or spasticity are present or if an anti-convulsant is needed. Diazepam can be given rectally but not through a syringe driver; if the latter route is preferred the water-soluble benzodiazepine midazolam can be used. (10-40 mg./24 hrs, Amesbury, 1989)

Steroids

Although steroids are relatively contra-indicated in immunocompromised patients, they should not be withheld in those with terminal illness, as their use can improve well-being and appetite, and reduce symptoms associated with pyrexia, dyspnoea, cough, raised intra-cranial pressure, and oedema surrounding tumours.

Route of administration

If swallowing tablets is difficult, the use of liquid medicines or rectal preparations is helpful. As the patients are usually wasted, intramuscular injections should be avoided; they cause pain and drug absorption may be unduly rapid. Syringe drivers are a much better alternative, as they can be used to deliver a continuous subcutaneous infusion of drugs to give even control of pain, nausea, and fits.

Use of a syringe driver

Syringe drivers (Dover, 1987) are small, battery operated pumps which the patient carries in a holster. They are usually refilled daily. The contents are delivered to the patient via a fine plastic tube connected to a small (25G) butterfly needle, which is inserted subcutaneously into the abdominal wall, anterior chest, arm or thigh. A loop of the tube is taped to the skin, and the needle site covered with a transparent dressing to allow inspection of the surrounding skin. Needles generally need resiting every 3-4 days, depending on the drugs used, some substances being more irritant than others.

A syringe driver is useful in patients:

1) who cannot take or refuse oral medication
2) with intractable diarrhoea and vomiting
3) with severe pain

Drugs used

1) Opioids

Diamorphine is the drug of choice, as it is more water-soluble than morphine. If the patient has already been taking oral morphine the daily starting dose of subcutaneous diamorphine should be one third that of the daily dose of morphine. If the patient has not been taking an opioid a low dose of diamorphine, e.g. 15mg/24 hours should be started, and increased as necessary to control symptoms.

2) Antiemetics

Antiemetics, can be given rectally (e.g. prochlorperazine) or added to the syringe driver. Useful centrally-acting antiemetics are haloperidol, cyclizine and methotrimeprazine. Haloperidol (5mg/24 hrs, increased as necessary) is well tolerated subcutaneously. Metoclopramide (20mg-60mg/24 hrs) can be added if vomiting persists. Cyclizine (50mg-100mg/24 hrs) is also effective but must be well diluted with sterile water or it crystallises. Methotrimeprizine (25-50 mg/24 hrs) is very sedative and so useful if this effect is required.

3) Hyoscine

Hyoscine hydrobromide is useful to dry up secretions, for example in terminal pneumonia, or for patients with colic. The dose is 0.4mg-2.0mg/24 hrs.

Babies and children with AIDS

Paediatric AIDS is an increasing problem; it has been estimated that by 1991 most new cases of AIDS in the world will be in children (Bradbeer, 1989). Most infants with HIV infection have acquired this in utero or at birth from their infected mothers, and so the management of the child's illness must include consideration of other family members.

If the child is the first member of the family to become unwell and be tested for HIV, the mother may have to confront not only the diagnosis of a fatal illness in her child, but, in addition the fact that she, and perhaps her partner and other children, are also likely to be infected. If the mother is already unwell from HIV disease she may be physically unable to care for her sick child, and feelings of inadequacy and guilt are then added to the grief associated with the child dying.

Poor social circumstances may also be present and contribute to the difficulties encountered by the family and those looking after them. These will be exacerbated by factors such as drug misuse or isolation. The latter is an especially common problem amongst immigrants from Africa, who are often unwilling to confide in other expatriates for fear of news of their diagnosis reaching their families. Isolation can also result from divided loyalties; for example, a woman who suspects that she caught HIV from her partner may fear that he will be ostracised if she tells her family about her condition.

The clinical features of AIDS in babies and young children can differ from those of adults, and so in 1987 the Centre for Disease Control in Atlanta, Georgia, USA, developed a separate classification system for HIV infection in children under 13 years of age. Infants with AIDS may suffer from all of the opportunistic infections seen in adults, but also present with recurrent serious bacterial infections including pneumonia, meningitis, abscesses, and ear, bone and joint infections. Another common feature in children is lymphoid interstitial pneumonitis which is characterised by persistent cough that cannot be attributed to the usual infections, and may require steriod treatment. Progressive neurological disease is also seen, and includes developmental regression, impaired brain growth, and progressive symmetrical motor deficits leading to paresis, ataxia, and walking difficulties.

Although home care is generally preferable for the child who is dying, admission to hospital will be indicated at times. Problems can then arise if parents of other patients on the paediatric ward know or suspect the diagnosis of the child dying with AIDS and express fears or prejudices towards the affected child and his family. Strict adherence to the rules of confidentiality is of course essential and the most delicate handling of this sort of situation is required. This may or may not include nursing the child in a single room, which is rarely required for infection control purposes.

If both mother and child are unwell and need hospital admission, it is usually desirable for them to remain together. Special arrangements will need to be made, determined by the illnesses of the individual patients and the local facilities, and requiring good liaison between the two or more specialist teams involved. Out-patient appointments will also need to be carefully planned to avoid unnecessary hospital visits; ideally the mother will be present whilst her child is seen, but the child entertained elsewhere when the mother's turn comes, so that she can feel free to discuss her problems and express her feelings without distraction.

Fear, stigmatisation and prejudice are also commonly encountered in the community care of the child with AIDS. Siblings, as well as the sick child, suffer rejection and social isolation, and therefore support given to the child and his family must take into account this added dimension on top of the normal grieving process.

The health visitor has a central role to play in the support of the family. This can be immensely time-consuming and emotionally taxing, bearing in mind all the potential difficulties already mentioned. It is usually necessary to refer to another agency or self-help group for additional specialised help.

The social worker can ensure that the family receives all the relevant state benefits and practical help to assist in the care of the child, and the occupational therapist may be needed to arrange adaptations to the home to accommodate the sick child, especially if he becomes wheelchair-bound.

The general practitioner, together with paediatric home nurses or general district nurses, will endeavour to alleviate all physical problems and to control pain. This may require close liaison with the paediatrician.

Just as for adults dying with AIDS, the continuing care of the child with advanced AIDS must be based on teamwork and co-operation between all the agencies involved, working together with the child and his family towards common goals.

References
Amesbury, BDW, 'The use of subcutaneous midazolam in the home care setting.' *Palliative Medicine*, 1989, pp. 299-301.

Bradbeer, C, Mothers with HIV. *British Medical Journal (BMJ)* 1989; 299: pp. 806-7 (Leader).

Dover, S, 'Syringe driver in terminal care,' *BMJ*, 1987, 294, pp. 553-555.

Chapter 3

COMMON DISTRESSING
SYMPTOMS AND TREATMENT

This chapter is a guide to symptom control in patients with AIDS. It does not discuss active management of opportunistic infections and tumours. These are comprehensively covered by other publications listed in the appendix. Good symptom control is important in promoting rapid recovery from such problems, but is most important for patients in the late stages of disease for whom active intervention is no longer generally appropriate.

Additional space has been left at the end of each table and the chapter to incorporate your own notes.

Table I: DIGESTIVE SYSTEM

The digestive system is a common source of distressing symptoms for people with AIDS. The most frequent are oral soreness, poor appetite, weight loss, and diarrhoea. Future problems can be prevented by attention to oral hygiene and nutrition before the patient becomes unwell, and the assistance of interested dentists and dieticians can be invaluable. Lack of money is a common reason for poor nutrition; a social worker may be able to obtain statutory or voluntary financial assistance, and some patients tolerate prescribable food supplements well.

Section 1: Mouth and throat

Dietary advice is a useful adjunct to specific treatment. Mouth soreness is helped by avoiding food that is acidic, spicy, or very hot or cold, and by the provision of soft, moist foods such as eggs or puddings. If swallowing is difficult, moist, homogenous foods such as mashed potatoes, porridge, or liquid dietary supplements are best tolerated.

Condition: Oral candidosis

Diagnosis: White patches on normal or red mucosa - can be removed with spatula; may cause red mucosa without plaques
Treatment: Amphotericin 10mg lozenges 4-8 per day, or nystatin mixture, 1 ml. qid (if severe or unresponsive to topical Rx then systemic Rx required, which may need to be continued indefinitely to prevent recurrences. Patients can usually titrate the dose required against symptoms & may need only 50 mg. fluconazole 1 x week); fluconazole 50 mg od for 1/52 initially (can be increased up to 400 mg od if necessary); or ketoconazole 200mg od-bd

Oesophageal candidosis

Diagnosis: Suspect if pharyngeal plaques are present or dysphagia co-exists with oral candidosis (occasionally occurs in the absence of overt oral infection).
No investigations necessary unless patient fails to respond to treatment.
Treatment: Systemic treatment with fluconazole or ketoconazole as above

Angular cheilitis

Diagnosis: Painful cracking at corners of mouth - usually candidal but staphylococcal infection may supervene
Treatment: 1% clotrimazole cream or 2% miconazole cream +/- 1% hydrocortisone cream.
Treat oral candidosis if present.
If staphylococcal infection suspected add mupirocin 2% ointment tds

Gingivitis

Diagnosis: Painful bleeding gums with erosions - often recurrent
Treatment: Metronidazole (400 mg tid x 5/7) or penicillin V 500   mg qid x 5/7
Dental hygiene.
Antiseptic mouth wash e.g. povidone-iodine 1%

Dental abscess

Diagnosis: Pain and swelling in jaw
Treatment: Antibiotics as for gingivitis.
Urgent dental referral

Aphthous ulceration

Diagnosis: Extremely painful ulcers in mouth or oesophagus - usually multiple
Treatment: Topical steroids e.g. adcortyl in Orabase (R) paste applied qid, hydrocortisone lozenges 2.5mg qid; benzydamine 0.15% mouthwash 2 hrly.
Thalidomide reported (Youle, M., etc. 1988)[1] as useful in resistant cases

Stomatitis

Diagnosis: Sore mouth with erythema and erosions. Can result from herpes infection. When painful blisters and ulcers on lips and in mouth are present, CMV, or follow radiotherapy
Treatment: TIf herpetic, oral acyclovir 200-400mg 5x/day for 1/52.
If nutritional status is poor, supplement vitamin B complex, C, and zinc
Clean teeth after each meal with a soft brush or cotton buds
Clean mouth every 2 hours with normal saline or hydrogen peroxide. Keep lips moist with petroleum jelly or lip salve
Avoid irritants such as alcohol, tobacco, and spicy foods
Benzydamine 0.15% mouthwash 2 hrly
Analgesia may be necessary to ensure adequate food intake

If extremely severe, consider tube feeding to improve nutritional state and allow healing

Xerostomia

Diagnosis: Dry mouth may be idiopathic or result from drugs, local radiotherapy, or low fluid intake in the terminally ill patient
Treatment: Strongly flavoured lozenges, sugar-free gum, and sorbet help increase salivation
Encourage high fluid consumption by frequent sips (avoid high sugar consumption as with xerostomia, dental caries is likely)
Brush teeth gently with a soft brush after each meal
Rinse mouth regularly with warm saline or non-alcoholic mouthwashes e.g. 0.5% chlorhexidine in water
Artificial saliva (Glandosane (R) prn); keep lips moist with petroleum jelly or lip salves

Oral hairy leukoplakia

Diagnosis: Painless, corrugated firmly adherent white patches on side of tongue and/or buccal mucosa
Treatment: Not generally required. If painful this is likely to be due to co-existent oral candidosis requiring treatment
Notes:

[1] Youle, M. Clarbour, J, Wade, P., Farthing, C, **AIDS: Therapeutics in HIV Disease,** Churchill Livingstone 1988, p. 46.

Section 2: Nausea and vomiting

Nausea and vomiting are common problems in patients with advanced disease. Drugs, e.g. high dose co-trimoxazole are the most likely causes and patients should eat before taking drugs that cause nausea. Small, frequent meals of low-fat, bland or salty foods are best tolerated. Gastrointestinal infections may also cause nausea and vomiting, usually in conjunction with diarrhoea. Vomiting may also result from mechanical causes such as gut lymphomas, and from raised intracranial pressure secondary to space-occupying lesions such as cerebral lymphoma.

Condition: nausea and vomiting

Diagnosis: Review medication, and consider treatable causes
Treatment: Standard anti-emetics can be used, but adverse effects are common
Metoclopramide 10mg tid po; prochlorperazine 5-10mg po 6 hrly prn; 25mg pr 6 hrly prn; if ineffective try nabilone 1-2mg bd po; Anti-emetics given an hour before meals may encourage an adequate food intake.
In terminally ill patients haloperidol, metoclopramide, cyclizine, or methotrimeprazine can be given through a syringe driver with other drugs (see Chapter 2)
Notes:

Section 3: Diarrhoea

Persistent diarrhoea can be caused by a wide variety of infections, drugs, and HIV enteropathy. Specific anti-infective agents are available for some infections, but often the diarrhoea persists despite treatment. Diarrhoea is commonly associated with malabsorption, and therefore oral treatment with anti-diarrhoeal tablets such as loperamide or codeine phosphate may be unhelpful. Patients should be advised to drink plenty of water and fruit juice, and to avoid foods high in fat, lactose, fibre, and caffeine.

Diarrhoea

Diagnosis: Consider infection and review medication
Treatment: As giardiasis is a common cause it is worth considering an empirical course of metronidazole 400 mg tid x 7/7.
If oral Rx tolerated try loperamide 4mg stat followed by 15mg after each loose stool up to 16mg/day or codeine phosphate 15-60mg every 4-6 hours; if these fail, and patient highly symptomatic, try morphine elixir 5-20mg po until diarrhoea controlled, and then switch to the same total daily dose of MST continuus (R) 10-20mg bd (see Chapter 2).
For intractable diarrhoea use a continuous sub-cutaneous infusion of diamorphine via a syringe driver
Notes:

Section 4: Anorexia and weight loss

Anorexia can result from drugs, HIV infection alone, other infections, or depression. The anti-retroviral drug zidovudine usually increases appetite, but may cause anorexia secondary to nausea. The help of a dietician is invaluable in planning a diet which encourages appetite and gives nutritional support, for example, small, frequent meals with food supplements in between. Megestrol acetate (a progesterone) helps some cachectic patients gain weight, but reduces libido.

Anorexia, weight loss

Diagnosis: Review medication, and consider depression
Treatment: Dietary advice.
Consider megestrol acetate, 80mg bd-qid
Avoid intramuscular injections in wasted patients
Notes:

Table II: SKIN PROBLEMS

Skin problems, particularly dry skin, are virtually universal in late disease, and can cause a great deal of discomfort.

Condition: Xeroderma

Diagnosis: Itchy, dry skin which is often cracked. Commonly associated with malabsorption
Treatment: Soap substitute + bath additive + moisturiser
Try alternative preparations if initial one ineffective or disliked.
Soap substitute e.g. emulsifying ointment or aqueous cream.
Bath additive e.g. Alpha Keri (R) bath oil or Oilatum Emollient (R).
Moisturiser e.g. E45 Cream (R) or emulsifying ointment

Seborrheic dermatitis

Diagnosis: Diffuse lesions of yellowish greasy scales on background of erythema: central face, scalp, chest, interscapular areas and groins. May become secondarily infected
Treatment: Face/body: use topical mixture of anti-infective agent and corticosteroid e.g. Vioform HC (R) (clioquinol + hydrocortisone) od-bd or Canesten HC (R) (clotrimazole + hydrocortisone).
If fails, use 2% ketoconazole cream or a 10/7 course of oral antifungal eg fluconazole 50 mg od or ketoconazole 200 mg od
Scalp: polytar (R) shampoo

Psoriasis

Diagnosis: Erythematous areas with silvery scaling.; may occur for the first time with immunosuppression
Treatment: Face/flexures: bd 1% hydrocortisone cream or Tarcortin (R)
Extensor surfaces: Tarcortin (R) bd + 10% salicylic acid nocte if hyperkeratotic
Scalp: polytar (R) shampoo

Tinea corporis/cruris/pedis

Diagnosis: Spreading, scaly, erythematous lesions on body, groins, or feet
Treatment: Topical antifungals e.g. clotrimazole 1% or miconazole 2%

Drug rashes

Diagnosis: Generalised erythematous itchy rash starting days after new medication More common and severe in patients with AIDS
Treatment: Stop drug if possible
Crotamiton 10% cream
Antihistamines e.g. terfanadine 60 mg bd + chlorpheniramine 4 mg nocte (sedative)

Molluscum contagiosum

Diagnosis: Pearly papules up to 5 mm in diameter on face and trunk .
May itch or be disliked for cosmetic reasons
Treatment: Cryotherapy or currettage and cautery

Folliculitis

Diagnosis: Small, papular or pustular, often itchy lesions on face, chest, axillae, upper arms and legs
May be bacterial or fungal or inflammatory
Treatment: Povidone-iodine 4% washes + oxytetracycline 250mg qds x 2/52 or minocycline 50mg po bd.
If itching a problem add oral antihistamines e.g. terfenadine 60 mg bd + chlorpheniramine 4 mg nocte (sedative).
If necessary, add strong topical corticosteroids e.g. betamethasone 0.1% bd-tid

Scabies

In immunocompromised patients enormous numbers of mites may be present. The rash may appear atypical with nodule formation and is highly infectious; other patients and nursing staff are often infected. Scabies should be considered in the differential diagnosis of any itchy rash in an AIDS patient
Diagnosis: Extremely itchy rash, with scales and crusts, which spares the face. Diagnosis can be confirmed by microscopy of a mite and/or ova removed from a burrow with a scalpel or fine needle
Treatment: If mild ,1% lindane applied to whole body but not head, and left for 24 hours. Repeat treatment after 1/52.
If severe, lindane 1% or malathion 0.5% may need to be applied weekly for several months.
Pruritus may be relieved by 10% crotamiton cream; if not add a strong topical steroid such as betamethasone 0.1% bd
Treat contacts (including staff at risk) with 1 application of lindane 1%

Impetigo and cellulitis.

Diagnosis: Often caused by a mixed infection with streptococci and staphylococci. Tender, hot, erythematous areas involving skin and/or deep tissues. May occur de novo or complicate a previous skin problem
Treatment: Mild impetigo may respond to 2% mupirocin ointment tid
If more severe, or cellulitis, use ampicillin 250mg- 500mg qid +
flucloxacillin 250mg - 500mg qid or erythromycin 500 mg qid for at least 2 weeks.

Herpes zoster (shingles)

Diagnosis: Painful, vesicular lesions on erythematous base involving one or more dermatome. Post-herpetic neuralgia occurs occasionally.
Treatment: Acyclovir 800mg 5x/day for 1 week (can be given intravenously but this may not be indicated for the dying patient)
Carbamazepine may reduce pain in some patients (100mg bd increasing up to 800mg/day).
Analgesia as necessary: opioids may be required
Treat post-herpetic neuralgia with amitriptyline, 10-25mg nocte increasing until relief occurs or side-effects become a problem (maximum dose 150mg) + analgesics as necessary e.g. dihydrocodeine 30mg 4 hrly prn.
Notes:

Table III: GENITAL, ANAL AND PERIANAL PROBLEMS

Genital discomfort is a frequent problem for people with AIDS; anal and perianal problems are common in homosexual patients but rare in other groups.

Herpes simplex infections

Diagnosis: Recurrent genital or perianal vesicles or ulcers. Defaecation painful if anus involved
Treatment: Oral acyclovir 200-400mg 5x/day for 5 days

Prophylaxis with 200-400mg bd may be necessary to prevent frequent recurrences

Candidosis

Diagnosis: Itching, erythema, +/- oedema and fissuring involving the genital and/or perianal area
Treatment: Topical antifungals e.g. 1% clotrimazole cream bd-tid (+ clotrimazole pessaries 200mg nocte x 3 for vulvovaginitis)
Notes:

Table IV: KAPOSI'S SARCOMA

Kaposi's sarcoma is a multifocal tumour which can occur anywhere in the skin, gastrointestinal tract, and viscera. In many patients only a few skin lesions are present, treatment is not required, and the patient eventually dies from other causes. In a few patients Kaposi's sarcoma progresses inexorably. Lung involvement causes persistent, progressive dyspnoea and cough. Lesions in the gastrointestinal tract can cause bleeding, pain, or obstruction, e.g. dysphagia from oesophageal involvement. Extensive skin lesions are associated with oedema, which can be aggravated by involvement of deep lymph nodes, e.g. in the inguinal canal.

The patient who is dying from extensive Kaposi's sarcoma has usually already received a great deal of chemotherapy and radiotherapy. Even if this is no longer having much effect on the tumour, the patient may wish to continue with systemic chemotherapy as he feels that it is reducing the rate of progression, or he may want treatment to individual lesions for cosmetic or symptomatic reasons. Steroids reduce the symptoms of systemic disease and the side-effects of chemotherapy and radiotherapy, and improve well-being; they are a useful adjunct to care for the dying patient.

Chemotherapy:

a) intralesional: Pre-treat skin with ethyl chloride spray. Inject 0.1 - 0.2 ml of vinblastine 0.3 mg/ml into centre of lesion.

b) systemic: If indicated, use bleomycin 15 - 30 mg i.v. (avoid if neotropenic or thrombocytopenic).

Radiotherapy:

Local radiotherapy may be useful for symptomatic lesions on the tip of the nose, conjunctiva, ears, or genitals, or for invasive lesions elsewhere resulting in oedema. Radiotherapy to the mouth should be given with caution as severe mucositis is common.

Facial KS

Treatment: Camouflage make-up (usually available from local department of dermatology).
Consider radiotherapy or intralesional chemotherapy.

Pulmonary KS

Treatment: If symptoms severe consider corticosteroids e.g. prednisolone 40mg or dexamethasone 6 mg mane, titrated against symptoms.
If patient wheezy, salbutamol inhaler 2 puffs qid
If pleuritic pain, non-steroidal anti-inflammatory drug e.g. naproxen 250-500mg bd.
Dyspnoea may sometimes be helped by a diuretic e.g. frusemide 20 mg. mane; codeine linctus 15-30mg tid-qid; or morphine e.g. MST continuus (R) 10mg bd (+ lactulose 15ml bd if necessary
Chemotherapy if requested by patient

Leg KS

Diagnosis: Invasive disease can result in oedema and deformity
Treatment: Encourage patient to elevate legs whenever possible
Elastic stockings
Obtain stick or wheelchair if necessary + any other aids required
Chemotherapy if requested by patient
If discomfort severe, add steroids and/or morphine as above

Necrotic ulceration

Diagnosis: Necrosis or diseased skin in terminally ill patient
Treatment: Clean with chloramine and paraffin or half strength hydrogen peroxide + mupirocin ointment tds.
If odour suggests anaerobic infection use metronidazole gel 0.8%
(Newman, V., 1989)[2]

Skin reactions following radiotherapy

Diagnosis: Erythema and desquamation in the weeks following radiotherapy
Treatment: Cover with dry, non adherent dressings, but expose area to air when practicable
1% hydrocortisone cream reduces itching
If moist desquamation is present cleanse area with half strength hydrogen peroxide and normal saline
Systemic antibiotics if secondary infection supervenes
Keep area dry . Advise loose clothing
Notes:

[2] Newman, V, The use of metronidazole gel to control the smell of malodorous lesion. **Palliatrive Medicine,** 1989, 3: pp 303-305.

Table V: RESPIRATORY TRACT

Pneumocystis carinii pneumonia (PCP) used to be by far the most common serious infection for AIDS patients in the western world. This is changing, as many centres now routinely give prophylaxis to all patients with HIV disease to prevent this infection. Consequently PCP is unlikely to be a problem in someone dying from AIDS unless prophylaxis has been discontinued. Death from PCP is rare except in patients who present with advanced disease which does not respond to treatment. Long term respiratory problems following PCP are uncommon unless the illness was exceptionally severe, when a persistent cough may ensue.

Bacterial pneumonias are common in people with AIDS, and may complicate pre-existing disease. PULmonary Kaposi's sarcoma causes progressive dyspnoea and cough (see above.) Lymphocytic interstitial pneumonia generally occurs in children, and is rare in adults. Failure to respond to steroids results in progressive respiratory failure.

Many patients with AIDS have persistent, mild but irritating respiratory symptoms related to other conditions, such as smoking, asthma, allergic rhinitis, or sinusitis, and treatment of these can be of great benefit.

NB. The diagnosis of PCP and other infections are not discussed. If a relatively well patient develops dry cough, fever and dyspnoea, further investigations must be considered.

Cough

Diagnosis: If productive consider superinfection
Treatment: Antibiotics if necessary e.g. doxycycline 200mg od then 100mg od for 9/7.
Codeine linctus 15-30mg tid-qid; or morphine eg MST continuus (R) 10mg bd + lactulose 15ml bd if necessary.
If severe, consider a short course of corticosteroids (e.g. prednisolone 40mg mane tapering over 10/7 and then stopped)

Dyspnoea

Treatment: If wheezy salbutamol inhaler 2 puffs qid.
Consider steroids e.g. prednisolone 20mg mane, titrated against symptoms.
Consider morphine e.g. MST continuus (R) 10-20mg bd + lactulose 15ml bd if necessary

Pleuritic pain

Diagnosis: May be associated with bacterial infection or Kaposi's sarcoma
Treatment: Non-steroidal anti-inflammatory drugs e.g. naproxen 250-500mg bd + analgesia if required (e.g. dihydrocodeine 30 mg 4 hrly prn + lactulose 15 ml bd if necessary)

Allergic rhinitis

Diagnosis: Nasal obstruction with sneezing. Post-nasal drip may cause coughing
Treatment: Betnesol (R) 2-3 drops into each nostril bd-tid, or Beconase (R) spray 2 puffs bd Sedative antihistamine at night if necessary e.g. chlorpheniramine 4mg
Notes:

Table VI: NEUROMUSCULAR PROBLEMS

Tiredness is the commonest complaint in people with AIDS. This may be associated with weakness, from myopathy associated with HIV disease or as a side effect of zidovudine. The most common and severe pain in AIDS patients is due to peripheral neuropathy, treatment of which is often unsatisfactory.

Tiredness

Diagnosis: Profound tiredness + hypersomnia. May be associated with persistent fever
Treatment: Consider depression.
Consider infection e.g. atypical mycobacteria.
Assess nutritional status.
Discuss ways of reducing stress and allowing more time for sleep e.g. if patient is still working a reduction in hours may help. Discourage too many late nights.
Support as necessary, e.g. home help, occupational therapy assessment.
If fever is present, with no treatable cause found, consider giving a small dose of corticosteroids (e.g. prednisolone 7.5-10mg mane, titrated against symptoms)

Peripheral neuropathy

Diagnosis: Symptoms usually in lower limbs. Patients describe 'burning' or 'tingling' with added sharp pains. Pain is increased by standing or walking

Treatment: Exclude treatable causes e.g. B12 deficiency.
Analgesics (including opiates) alone are usually unhelpful
Patients respond differently, and so experimentation may be needed
Try carbamazepine 100mg bd increased slowly up to 1.2g/day or sodium valproate 200 mg tds increased slowly up to 2.5g daily
If unsuccessful, add or substitute amitriptyline 10-25mg nocte increasing until symptoms improved or side effects become a problem (maximum dose 150mg nocte).
Also consider a non-steroidal anti-inflammatory drug e.g. naproxen 150-500mg bd or dihydrocodeine 30 mg 6hrly prn or morphine (eg MST continuus (R) 10-20mg bd)

Notes:

Table VII: EYE DISEASE

Cytomegalovirus (CMV) retinitis is a serious progressive manifestation of AIDS which frequently results in blindness. In a patient who has already suffered greatly, blindness can be unbearable, and suicides have been reported. The treatment of CMV retinitis is with intravenous ganciclovir through a permanent indwelling intravenous line. This needs to be continued as long as some sight remains even in a patient dying from other causes. Other eye symptoms are often readily treatable, and treatment can improve the quality of life considerably.

Blindness

Diagnosis: When patient can only count fingers

Treatment: Refer patient to consultant ophthalmologist for registration as blind (gives access to social worker for the blind, and provision of talking books, bus pass, TV licence, white stick, etc)

Conjunctivitis

Diagnosis: Painful, red, sticky eyes with blurred vision in the mornings
Treatment: Chloramphenicol eye drops for 2/52
False tears e.g. hypromellose if discomfort persists

Double vision

Diagnosis: Usually due to extraocular muscle palsy
Treatment: Consider treatable infection especially cryptococcal meningitis
Cover either eye with a pirate patch or scarf to relieve symptoms

Difficulty reading

Diagnosis: Presbyopia or hypermetropia is often more difficult to cope with in ill people
Treatment: See optician for prescription of stronger reading glasses. Advise use of a strong light for reading
Notes:

Table VIII: CEREBRAL DISEASE

The brain in AIDS patients can be affected by opportunistic infections, neoplasms, and HIV itself. Effective treatment is available for most infections, but symptoms due to raised intracranial pressure or meningism may persist. The prognosis for patients with cerebral lymphoma is extremely poor, even if treatment with readiotherapy is given. Severe HIV encephalopathy is common in the last days or weeks of life, but rare before this.

Headaches

Diagnosis: May follow investigations e.g. lumbar puncture or be symptomatic of cerebral involvement with HIV or other infections, or space-occupying lesions.
Can be unrelated to AIDS e.g. caused by muscular tension or drugs
Treatment: Quiet surroundings, avoid bright lights
Analgesia e.g. dihydrocodeine 30mg 4 hrly prn (+ lactulose 15ml bd if necessary).
If severe or evidence of raised intracranial pressure consider corticosteroids e.g. dexamethasone (10mg mane until pain controlled and then reducing)

Convulsions

Diagnosis: Can occur with space occupying lesions or in terminal disease with encephalopathy
Treatment: Quiet surroundings, avoid bright lights
Control fits with diazepam 10mg pr (Stesolid (R), repeated after 5 minutes if necessary.
If long term treatment necessary, give oral anti-epileptic e.g. carbamazepine (100mg bd increasing over 1-2/52 up to 1.2g/day)
If patient terminal, control fits with rectal diazepam or subcutaneous midozalam via a syringe driver (Chapter 2)

HIV encephalopathy

Diagnosis: Usually insidious onset in late disease, initially characterised by poor memory and concentration, apathy and withdrawal, and ataxia, later disinhibition, global dementia, paralysis, and incontinence can occur. Patients may alternate between confusion and fear.
Aggression is uncommon except in patients who have had previous psychiatric illness.
Treatment: Consider depressive illness; if likely add a stimulant anti-depressant e.g. flupenthixol (1mg mane initially increasing up to 3mg mane)
Consider other treatable causes e.g. alcohol, hypoxia, medication; provide quiet, unchanging, surroundings and reassurance.
The presence of a soft light and a clock at all times and familiar faces improve orientation
If agitated or psychotic, sedate as necessary e.g. chlorpromazine 25mg-50mg po.
Consider psychiatric review
If hallucinating use haloperidol (0.5-1mg bd, increased as necessary) or trifluoperazine (1mg bd, increased as necessary)
Notes:

Table IX: PSYCHOLOGICAL PROBLEMS

Sadness, anger, anxiety and guilt are common feelings in people dying from AIDS. These reactions may be an appropriate response, in which case skilled counselling is often of great value. Depressive illness also occurs frequently and should be looked for as disturbances in sleep, appetite and mood can be reversed by treatment.

Insomnia

Treatment: Determine sleep pattern, and whether the patient is worrying about anything in particular.
Suggest avoidance of caffeine and other stimulants in the evenings.
A counsellor or psychologist can provide any counselling indicated, as well as relaxation exercises.
If clinical depression present, give amitryptiline 25 mg one hour before retiring, increased to 50 mg 3/7 later and increased further 3/7 later if necessary
Hypnotics e.g. temazepam 10-20mg nocte may be useful for a few nights e.g. if a patient is bereaved, but long term use should be avoided as they are addictive and depressant.

Depression

Diagnosis: Sleep disturbance, often with early waking, poor appetite, feeling depressed
Treatment: If sleep is poor use a sedative antidepressant e.g. amitrityline 25mg nocte, increased after 3/7 to 50 mg nocte and increased further as necessary.
If patient lethargic try flupenthixol, initially 1 mg mane increasing up to 3 mg mane.
Refer to counsellor or psychologist for support
Notes:

Continuation note -page for entire chapter.

Chapter 4

HOSPITAL-BASED CARE

Who should look after people with HIV?

The diagnosis of HIV infection may be made by doctors working in many different fields. Most asymptomatic people who are worried about HIV attend for counselling and testing at the relevant hospital clinic, such as the department of genito-urinary medicine or drug dependency unit. Some, however, prefer to ask their general practitioners. Ill patients may have the diagnosis of HIV infection made as the result of an emergency admission, for example with pneumocystis carinii pneumonia (PCP), or in the course of routine investigation, perhaps by a gastroenterologist looking for the cause of non-specific symptoms such as pyrexia and weight loss, or by an oncologist who has identified an unusual lymphoma. The diagnosis may also be made by other health care workers; for example, Kaposi's sarcoma of the mouth is often found by dentists.

Once the patient knows that he has HIV infection, and has been counselled about this, then future medical care must be discussed. As the management of people with HIV improves it becomes increasingly important for such patients to have access to a specialist unit. Most clinics which offer a service for testing will have links with such a unit, and patients will be referred to it as a matter of course. If the test has been carried out elsewhere the patient should still be referred to a specialist in HIV infection. There is generally no need for him to continue to attend other hospital departments unless he has a condition which requires specialist treatment, for example a lymphoma. Obviously it is important, however, for the patient to continue to see his general practitioner.

The optimal management of an individual patient depends on a number of factors, particularly co-existing conditions such as haemophilia or drug addiction, and social circumstances. Provision of care also varies between different health districts. Most people with HIV infection are looked after by one or more of the following:-

Departments of Genito-Urinary Medicine

In the United Kingdom most people known to have HIV infection are male homosexuals. These men have often already attended a department of genito-urinary medicine (GUM) intermittently for years with a variety of sexually transmitted infections; some of these, such as herpes, warts, syphilis, and hepatitis B, can recur in an immunocompromised patient. Much of the out-patient management of these patient is concerned with treating such infections, and related activities in which genito-urinary physicians have a major part, such as tracing and testing contacts. In the majority of districts genito-urinary physicians now have the most experience and best facilities for looking after out-patients with HIV, and see most infected patients. As few GUM departments have access to beds, however, other arrangements must be made for patients who need admission.

Drug dependency units

In many parts of the country the number of people infected with HIV as a result of drug misuse is increasing rapidly. Such individuals are often chaotic, making management extremely difficult. Drug dependency units (DDUs) therefore have a vital role in the care of those who continue to misuse drugs. Even if these patients need to attend other departments for the treatment of medical conditions, it usually simplifies matters if psychoactive drugs are only prescribed by the DDU.

Haematologists

Haemophiliacs have often attended a particular haemophilia centre for many years, and continue to have haematological problems. As they became infected as a result of medical treatment they are unlikely to feel any affinity with people who acquired the infection by other routes, and indeed may blame them for contaminating the supply of blood products. For these reasons most haemophiliacs remain under the care of haematologists, usually in a separate department from other groups with HIV infection.

Infectious disease units

Infectious disease (ID) units would seem to be ideal for the management of both in-patients and out-patients with HIV. Over the last twenty years many British units have closed, however, and as the remainder are widely scattered there may be no convenient unit for an individual patient. The units that remain have now generally built up a considerable body of expertise, and see a large proportion of local people with HIV.

Out-patient care

Asymptomatic HIV-positive patients generally attend for an out-patient assessment every three months or so; ill patients may be seen as necessary which can occasionally be as often as several times in a week. As many patients have multiple problems these visits are usually lengthy, perhaps lasting thirty minutes. In parts of the country where the prevalence of HIV is low it is usually impossible to have a dedicated unit for the few infected patients, although it may be feasible to arrange a regular weekly session in which a counsellor and social worker are also available.

If patient numbers justify a dedicated out-patient unit this can be of great value, as those attending feel that they have a secure place to visit in which they will not be stigmatised. The knowledge that the unit can always offer help not only improves morale, but also gives opportunity for the early diagnosis and treatment of illness.

Many conditions, such as mild PCP, can now be managed in out-patients departments, although facilities for ready admission to hospital if necessary must be available. The patients will not only meet each other informally, but can be put in touch with others with similar problems for mutual support. This is also helpful if someone is uncertain about starting new therapy, as he can hear what it is like from someone who has experienced it. It is essential, however, to avoid burdening the 'perfect patient'.

Design of an out-patient unit

As many patients are worried about confidentiality it is helpful if the entrance to the clinic is not in the busiest part of the hospital, and if its name is neutral and uninformative. Patients will feel more secure in pleasant surroundings, and charitable funds are often available for the reception area to have comforts such as a coffee maker, plants, and pictures. Educational material can also be on display. In addition to the reception area, consulting rooms and lavatory facilities, one or more treatment rooms are essential. These should be equipped with reclining chairs so that chemotherapy and blood transfusions can be given, and a couch for minor procedures.

In large units it may be possible to staff a 'drop-in' clinic, but most units will need to run an appointment system. This must not only include provision for emergencies but also be flexible in order to encourage early presentation. This can be assisted by giving an information sheet to the patients, outlining when the clinic is open, how emergency and routine appointments can be made, and how patients can obtain other services, for example, a repeat prescription when they have run out of medication.

Chaotic patients commonly fail to keep appointments and instead present only when they have medical and social problems, often at the most inconvenient times. If this causes frequent disruption it may become necessary to make rules about the use of the clinic by such patients, perhaps stating that they will only be seen by appointment, and if they appear without one they will need to wait for the next available time or be seen elsewhere, for example in a routine genito-urinary medicine clinic or in the Accident and Emergency (A&E) department. These rules should be made known to the patients, and agreed and adhered to by all members of staff to avoid manipulation.

Role of different staff members

Reception staff

The receptionist is not only likely to be the first person the patient meets in the unit, but will also coordinate much of his future care. He or she therefore needs to be welcoming, have a good memory for names, and be unflappable. Patients often confide in reception staff; as this can be stressful it is helpful if the receptionist has good support outside work, perhaps from the spouse or from firm religious beliefs. Training about confidentiality must be provided, as should some education in the natural history and management of AIDS.

Doctors

As people with HIV infection often have complex medical and social problems it is simpler if they can see the same doctor on each occasion. If someone is acutely ill this may not be possible, but otherwise can generally be arranged. The resultant close doctor-patient relationship is usually valuable in supporting the patient, but may cause problems when, for example, a doctor moves on to another job.

Patients with especially complex conditions may also need to see specialists, most frequently dermatologists, radiotherapists, ophthalmologists, neurologists, psychiatrists, and ear, nose and throat surgeons. Links with an individual specialist are beneficial, and if he is in great demand it may be possible for him to do a regular clinic in the HIV unit.

This will not only improve his experience of HIV infection, but also enable him to teach the clinic doctors.

Nurses

Nurses also establish close relationships with the patients, and this can be encouraged by planning for the same nurse to assist at the clinics of an individual doctor. As the nurse may be asked to carry out many different practical procedures, wide experience is useful, and additional training in infection control, use of nebulisers, and intravenous treatment, may also be required.

Administrative staff

A dedicated unit will need its own secretarial and clerical back-up, which may include computerisation. It may be possible for two individuals to alternate between secretarial and reception work, which will help to reduce stress. Training in confidentiality and an outline of the management of AIDS patients is obviously essential.

Health advisers/Counsellors

Patients should see a trained counsellor before their HIV test, and again after they have been found positive. After this, most of their counselling can usually be informal, and given by doctors and other staff. At times of crisis, however, patients may again profit from more specific and lengthy counselling and support, and so provision for this is important. Health advisers also help by providing practical care information, and can direct individual patients towards the support groups and other resources which are likely to be of most benefit to them.

Psychologists

The role of the psychologist varies between different clinics, and the special interests of the individual practitioner. Access to an interested psychologist is particularly useful for those patients who have major problems in coming to terms with HIV and AIDS and for those with anxiety and depression all of whom may need additional support. It is often difficult to differentiate between the changes of early HIV encephalopathy and the symptoms of anxiety and depression, and in these cases the assessment of a psychologist may be of great benefit.

Social workers

People with HIV infection often have many social problems, ranging from difficulties with relationships to unsatisfactory housing or being sent to prison. Although problems such as poverty are most likely to be severe when someone has become chronically unwell, some may surface much earlier. In addition, advice at the right time can prevent a course of action with unfortunate consequences, such as resigning from a job which has a linked entitlement to benefits in case of illness. For these reasons referral to a social worker at an early stage can be of great value. The social worker also helps the patient to obtain all the benefits to which he is entitled, and can coordinate the efforts of statutory and voluntary bodies to prevent duplication of applications for benefits and grants. The social worker performs a vital role in the care of the ill patient who wishes to stay at home, by supporting him and arranging and coordinating their community services.

Dieticians

Good nutrition is important in maintaining immune function and in symptom control, and the advice of an interested dietician can do much to help people in all stages of HIV infection.

Pharmacy

Polypharmacy commonly presents problems in the management of AIDS, and can result in complex drug interactions and side effects. Many of the drugs used are experimental, and need to be obtained directly from the pharmaceutical company concerned. The pharmacy can often give useful advice and help with these problems. In addition it may be possible for drugs for intravenous use to be reconstituted in sterile conditions in the pharmacy; this not only reduces the risk of septic complications but makes it easier and safer for the patient with cytomegalovirus retinitis to treat himself at home through a Hickman line.

In-patient care

It is becoming increasingly feasible to maintain ill people with AIDS in the community rather than by admitting them to hospital. Admission may sometimes be needed, however, for example for the diagnosis of a new illness, or while community care is being arranged.

If the out-patient unit has access to its own beds, patients will remain under the care of the same medical team, although much day to day treatment will be given by house staff new to the patient. The alternative is admitting patients under the care of another firm, usually that of the designated AIDS physician. If so, good liaison between out-patient and in-patient teams is essential so that major decisions about management can be discussed. This may be achieved by a combined weekly meeting, ward rounds attended by members of both teams, and informal discussions when necessary. In large units it may be possible to create a senior house officer or registrar post shared by the two groups, which will improve continuity of care.

Should there be a dedicated ward for AIDS patients? If patient numbers are large it may be possible for one or more entire wards to be reserved for them. If there are only a few HIV-positive in-patients at any one time they may either be admitted to one ward (cluster bedding) or spread throughout the hospital (scatter bedding). If all patients are on one ward its staff develop confidence and expertise, and there is no danger of patients being subjected to draconian infection control measures. It is also convenient for the patients' doctors and social workers. In addition the patients do not feel isolated, and may develop beneficial camaraderie.

One disadvantage of having a dedicated ward is that it can be stressful for both patients and staff, particularly during periods in which there are several deaths. Some patients may not wish to be admitted to the AIDS ward, perhaps because they fear that friends or family will hear where they are and guess the diagnosis. Other patients prefer not to be with others with AIDS, or may dislike a particular group such as homosexuals or drug users. In addition, staff on other wards develop no experience of AIDS, and so are not equipped to deal with the occasional patient who needs admission. Even if the majority of patients are admitted to the dedicated ward, special arrangements may need to be made for certain patients. The admission of a sick mother and baby is likely to create the most problems; the solution will depend upon their clinical state and the resources available.

Shortage of beds may not allow the luxury of choice, as patients will be admitted to any available bed. This can make ward rounds time consuming, but means that staff throughout the hospital lose their fear of dealing with people with AIDS. As the staff become more confident, the stigma of the disease declines.

Hospital staff who are likely to look after people with HIV need training in this, which can range from full-time courses lasting several weeks to local 'updates' of a few hours. Most of these are for nurses, but some are for other staff in contact with the patient, such as ward receptionists. Even if it is impossible to enable all staff to attend special courses, those that have can participate in informal teaching sessions for their colleagues.

Dying in hospital

Hospitals are generally busy, noisy places which aim to make people better; they are not designed primarily for dying people. People with AIDS can often now choose where they would like to die, and this will usually be at home or in a hospice. Those that die in hospital do so for a number of reasons. A few patients wish to stay at home for as long as possible, but to return to hospital to die among familiar faces. In some areas the alternatives of community or hospice care are not available. These options may be refused, perhaps by someone who has been unable to come to terms with dying. A patient with AIDS may present for the first time with advanced disease and die before a diagnosis is made, or fail to respond to treatment. Another patient may deteriorate quite suddenly while being investigated and treated for an acute illness, and by the time it becomes apparent that he is dying he may be too ill to be moved.

Good nursing is essential. This may be very demanding as people dying from AIDS often become comatose for the last week or so of life, and need turning every two hours to prevent skin necrosis. A side room will provide some privacy, and allow the patient to talk openly to his loved ones and those looking after him. Staff need to allow time for listening and answering questions, and a counsellor may be able to help the patient come to terms with his death and resolve any outstanding problems with his relationships. Continuity of care is important, particularly if the patient is confused. Doctors, nurses and perhaps also counsellors will also need to spend time with the patient's family and friends; this is often easier away from the ward, particularly if a partner decides that the time has come to confront his own health worries and be tested for HIV.

Deaths from AIDS in hospital can be distressing for ward staff, often because the patient has deteriorated suddenly, and neither the patient nor the staff have had time to come to terms with the death. Perhaps the most difficult occasions are when someone who was previously well becomes increasingly unwell from an undiagnosed condition, as it is difficult to know when to stop invasive investigations and perhaps empirical treatment, and concentrate on symptom control. There may also be a great sense of frustration and failure amongst the doctors and nurses. Staff morale may be adversely affected by a 'run' of deaths in one ward, for whatever reasons, and consideration should be given to providing additional support at this time. The morale and confidence of staff - and patient care - can be helped if some of the nurses are able to have special training in terminal care nursing.

Chapter 5

CARE IN THE COMMUNITY

Many people with AIDS choose to die at home or to spend some of their last weeks or months there. Their continuing care in terms of symptom control and physical and emotional support should be the same as for any other individual with a fatal condition. This can involve the general practitioner, district nurse and other community nurses, social services, and voluntary agencies. AIDS does, however, generate some additional problems which need specific attention.

The general practitioner

The role of the general practitioner in the continuing care of people with AIDS is often difficult, as many patients have received all their medical care at hospitals with specialist HIV services to the exclusion of the GP. This is due to a combination of factors. Firstly, since HIV infection has so far mainly affected previously healthy young men who have needed minimal medical attention be-fore developing AIDS, the patients have often not developed a relationship with their general practitioner, and may not even be registered with one. In addition some people with AIDS are reluctant to allow their GP to be informed of their diagnosis or HIV status, for fear of breaches of confidentiality within the surgery or wider community and/or of rejection or negative attitudes on the part of the doctor. However ill-founded these fears may be, they are very real for the patient, and are often based on personal or reported experiences.

Once the terminal stage of AIDS is reached it may be impossible or inappropriate for the patient to receive medical care at the hospital. Out-patient visits become too exhausting and in-patient care may not be indicated. The GP, in communication with the hospital doctors where necessary, is the most appropriate person to provide care at this time. Therefore it is advisable to encourage people with AIDS to establish a relationship with the GP early on in their illness, and it is essential that GPs can feel confident that the standards of confidentiality and infection control within the surgery are high.

The district nurse

The district nurse has a lot to offer, by way of expertise and knowledge of local services and amenities, in the continuing care of people with AIDS. Some health authorities have teams of specialist community nurses or individual nurse specialists for HIV and AIDS. Their roles vary according to the policy of each health authority and the number of patients with AIDS within it.

Although all district nurses must have a basic knowledge of HIV infection and AIDS, in parts of the country where the prevalence is very low it may be inappropriate to keep all community nurses highly trained in this area. Instead one or two may become 'specialists' who can mobilise services and resources quickly and train and support other staff when the need arises. On the other hand, where HIV infection and AIDS are more common, clinical nurse specialists, either working individually or in teams, may be needed to educate, advise and support the district nurses in all aspects of the care of people with AIDS, and to ensure a high standard and continuity of care.

Whatever the situation, every district nurse has a continuing responsibility to keep herself informed about HIV and AIDS including knowledge of local voluntary services, policies on infection control and confidentiality, and protocols for current treatment and symptom control. Since the only effective way of preventing blindness in cytomegalovirus retinitis is to give daily intravenous drugs for weeks or months, health authorities need to develop policies and training programmes to enable this treatment to be given by district nurses. At present these drugs are often administered by a friend of the patient, as the nurse is not allowed to do so despite her specific training. Even patients who can manage their own therapy benefit from the support of a suitably trained district nurse who can also monitor their physical and mental condition and ability to cope at home.

The home nursing care of someone with advanced AIDS is the same as for anyone else who is terminally ill, with symptom control, emotional and physical support of the patient and his loved ones, and maintenance of patient control and dignity as the highest priorities. Nursing equipment must also be supplied as necessary.

There are also features unique to AIDS which need consideration. In particular the amount of emotional support needed may be particularly high and very time consuming. Many people dying with AIDS are themselves grieving for the deaths of close friends and lovers. They may have feelings of guilt at having possibly infected others. Those caring for a person dying with AIDS may be viewing what they see as their own future. Stigmatisation and prejudice have caused isolation of many people with AIDS and rejection by relatives, friends, and neighbours. Changed body image due to weight loss or skin lesions and loss of self esteem due to inability to work, or even maintain independence, all cause low morale. Community nurses need to appreciate these and other individual factors and allow sufficient time to offer support or know where to refer the patient and his carers for appropriate help. They also need to recognise their own need for support, in whatever form, as caring for young dying patients is always emotionally as well as physically demanding.

Health visitors also provide support for people with AIDS especially when there are young children involved. This can also be extremely time consuming and emotionally draining and may be complicated by the problem of drug misuse in the family.

The community psychiatric nurse (CPN) can be a valuable resource in the care of those with a drug problem and for patients with encephalopathy. As well as providing specific care, the CPN's expertise and advice can help other carers to cope with these problems.

Social services

Other forms of practical help in the terminal care of someone with AIDS may come from the social services of the local authority, in particular the home help service. The 'meals-on-wheels' service and home carers may also be involved. Many local authorities have special training programmes on HIV and AIDS for their employees. These are essential for 'frontline' staff like home helps, home carers and meals-on-wheels servers to give them a good understanding of infection control and

confidentiality, and an opportunity to explore their attitudes to the various lifestyles of their clients so that they can be confident and compassionate in the service they provide.

Voluntary services

In many cases the statutory services are supplemented by voluntary help. The voluntary response to AIDS has been magnificent and there are now many organisations providing a wide range of practical help, financial assistance, counselling services, advice and support groups for people with AIDS. Many people feel more comfortable with the help of voluntary agencies than that of the statutory services, and also find the former more flexible. This is particularly true for male homosexuals since many of the volunteers are also gay. Some intravenous drug misusers are reluctant to accept social services because of a mistrust of such statutory organisations and the fear that their children will be taken into care by the social workers. In the majority of cases, however, a combination of statutory services, voluntary agencies and informed carers e.g. partners, friends and family, provides the best package of care for the person with advanced AIDS at home.

Working together

Co-operation and communication between the various carers is essential. This begins with good discharge planning from hospital, which should begin as soon as possible following admission. This can be managed by a regular multidisciplinary meeting on the ward or unit, which is attended by the liaison nurse or specialist community nurses. The patient and his carers are of course involved in discharge planning, and decisions to refer to statutory and voluntary services are made with them.

If a patient has advanced AIDS, the GP and district nurse should be involved as soon as possible so that useful relationships can be made before the patient is too severely ill. Where possible the district nurse should visit the patient in hospital before discharge, as this helps to reduce the apprehension the patient may have about going home, and about accepting the district nursing service. This also helps the district nurse, as she can start to develop a relationship with the patient, begin a nursing assessment, and arrange services and order any necessary equipment before the patient goes home.

Similarly good co-operation between the various community services is essential. In the care of some people with AIDS there can be several different agencies involved, with a confusing number of people visiting the home, resulting in a danger of overlap of services and, indeed, gaps and confusion of roles. For instance, a friend or partner may appear to be doing the same tasks as a home help. If the individuals concerned can meet, or liaise by telephone, the overlap between their roles can be identified, and gaps in provision filled, with minimum resentment for those involved and to the benefit of the patient.

Voluntary services are invaluable in providing night time care or company for the person at home with advanced AIDS. Many health authorities have no night district nursing service, although they may be able to provide a nurse for the last few nights of the terminally ill patient. The night is the most frightening time for people with AIDS and their carers, and this anxiety is not confined to the last few nights. District nurses need to be aware of the local voluntary services who can provide night care and should make appropriate referrals and maintain lines of communication with them. This may be via a written 'diary' kept in the home or by regular telephone or personal contact.

Good communication and co-operation should result in an atmosphere of teamwork, in which the patient is one of the team, but without jeopardising confidentiality.

Confidentiality

The obligation upon carers, statutory and voluntary, to maintain confidentiality applies to all patients, but needs to be stressed in the care of people with AIDS at home because of the generalised fear and prejudice within the community. This has been demonstrated by violence to people with AIDS, and their property, and by stigmatisation by neighbours, friends, colleagues and family.

Maintaining confidentiality in community care, whilst providing a comprehensive package of services, needs careful management. A policy on confidentiality should exist within every community service, including GP surgeries; such a policy should state who needs to know a patient's diagnosis and recognise that the patient's express permission must be gained before any information is divulged to another carer or community worker. These policies need to be backed by education of all staff to ensure that they are implemented, and that the implications of a breach of confidentiality are clearly understood.

Inadvertant breaches of confidentiality can easily occur in the community setting. For example, in the case of one terminally ill young man with AIDS, the district nurses recorded on the outside of the home nursing notes the name and telephone number of the Terence Higgins Trust. This advertised his diagnosis to anyone visiting him. Similarly, yellow plastic sacks of infected waste, left on the doorstep for collection, may indicate to neighbours that there is someone with HIV infection living there. Care should therefore be taken about what is recorded in the home nursing notes and in records kept in clinics, surgeries and offices since many people have access to these who do not need to know the diagnoses of patients or clients. It is necessary for the professional carers to clarify with the patient which of his friends and family are aware of the diagnosis, and make this information available to other members of the team.

Chapter 6

HOSPICE CARE

Hospices aim to improve the quality of life for the dying patient by good symptom control and emotional support. They provide the surroundings for someone to die comfortably, peacefully, and with dignity, and continuing support for the bereaved. In addition patients may be admitted for a short period, perhaps two weeks, of convalescence or respite care.

A period of convalescence is often helpful following a hospital admission for a severe acute illness, particularly when it is the patient's first diagnosis of AIDS, as it allows him time to recover, in restful surroundings, come to terms with his diagnosis, and perhaps adapt to changed circumstances such as visual impairment. Respite care allows the friends or family who have been looking after the patient to have a break from their responsibilities. It may also make future care in the community easier as it gives an opportunity for reassessment of the patient, so that symptom control may be improved and additional statutory or voluntary services arranged if necessary.

In London there are two hospices specifically designed for people with AIDS: the Mildmay Mission Hospital and the London Lighthouse. Both are funded by a combination of donations, grants, DSS allowances and contributions from the regional health authorities. They have both been designed and equipped following consultation with those who might use the service, and 'institutional' furniture has been avoided.

The Mildmay Mission Hospital

Mildmay is a Christian foundation, but aims to care for people without regard to race, creed, culture or lifestyle. The AIDS unit is part of a small charitable hospital in the East End of London; it also acts as a GP hospital for the local community, providing beds for convalescent and respite care as well as those for disabled and young chronic sick patients. Its philosophy is to restore control to the patient, and so the patients' wishes largely determine the choice of treatment.

People with AIDS may be admitted for terminal or respite care, or convalescence following a hospital stay for an acute illness. Patients have their own room and lavatory and washing facilities, access to a communal kitchen, dining and sitting area, and private rooms used for counselling. Medical and nursing staff place great emphasis on good symptom control, and counsellors also have a vital role in helping patients and their friends and relations. A welfare officer arranges and coordinates services for patients returning home, and a home care team has now been started to provide support in the community.

The Mildmay also has an education and training department which organises a variety of courses for health care workers and others interested in the care of people with AIDS.

The London Lighthouse

The London Lighthouse has been established to provide a range of services for people affected by HIV infection. In addition to the residential unit there are facilities for counselling and training, community services, and a drop-in centre and cafe which are open to the public.

The residential unit is used for convalescence, respite and terminal care. There are beds for 24 residents, six in single rooms and the remainder divided between four larger rooms; each room has an adjacent shower and lavatory. Residents are encouraged to determine their choice of medical and nursing care. There is also a communal sitting room and kitchen, as well as other rooms used for counselling and treatment. In addition the Lighthouse contains a mortuary, and funeral services can be carried out on site.

Extension of aid into the community is provided mainly by volunteers, who are trained to provide intensive domiciliary nursing help and support to ill people with AIDS and ARC.

A range of different counselling methods, support groups and information services are available at the Lighthouse for people with HIV infection. These include groups for drug users, haemophiliacs, and partners, families and friends of people with HIV. Other services include classes in relaxation, exercise, drama, and art, and complementary therapies such as hypnotherapy, massage, shiatsu, and reflexology.

General hospices

At the time of writing the Mildmay and the Lighthouse are the only hospices in England which cater specifically for AIDS patients. Outside London the availability of hospice care will depend on local facilities and attitudes. Many hospices rely on charitable funds given for the benefit of cancer patients, and may have been established specifically for the needs of this group. Such factors may cause difficulties in the admission of patients with AIDS.

Hospices have much to offer in management of people with AIDS, and we hope that in the future more hospices will be able to extend their services to these patients. Even in London general hospices have an important part to play, as some patients, particularly heterosexuals such as haemophiliacs and Africans, may prefer an institution perceived by them as being free from the stigma of AIDS.

There are many similarities between people with AIDS and those with cancer, both in the symptoms they present and in the treatment required, and so experienced hospice staff may find looking after people dying from AIDS less difficult than they anticipate. There are, however, some important differences. People with AIDS are often young, and may therefore have quite different expectations from those with cancer. There may be social factors associated with the lifestyle of individual patients. In addition the range of symptoms differs; severe pain can occur but is less common in AIDS patients than in those with solid tumours, whereas mucocutaneous discomfort caused by infections such as candida or herpes is much more common.

Confidentiality is another area in which there may be differences, as people with AIDS generally dislike their diagnosis being known to more than a few close friends and perhaps family. All members of staff may need to consider this, as inadvertant lapses can easily occur. For example a moment of carelessness on the telephone to one of the patient's acquaintances, or the mention of 'AIDS' on a death certificate may cause considerable distress to the patient or his family. Inappropriate infection control precautions such as 'danger of infection' notices or the over-liberal use of gowns, masks and gloves can alert other patients and result in gossip, and distress for the patient. Most people with AIDS can easily be safely nursed on an open ward with no overt precautions other than adherence to district guidelines when carrying out procedures involving exposure to body fluids.

Although it is now well established that the occupational risk of HIV infection is minimal, it is natural for health care workers who are inexperienced in this field to be apprehensive despite their knowledge. Their anxiety is often exacerbated by the attitudes of their families and friends, who are likely to be much less well-informed. Reducing these worries may take considerable education and reassurance; the most helpful approach may be to enable staff to spend a day with doctors or nurses working in an AIDS unit and so become familiar with the routine precautions used.

When it is decided that a hospice will accept AIDS patients, it may be necessary for some staff members to receive additional training in the management of these patients. Courses for this are mainly available in the large cities, particularly London, but local health districts now also provide education and 'update' sessions. Doctors and nurses working with AIDS patients will also welcome staff from hospices who wish to attend AIDS units, as exchange of ideas between the two groups must be of great benefit to our patients.

Chapter 7

DEATHS AND FUNERALS

When someone with AIDS dies there are certain points to note about the care of the body, the role of the undertakers and the funeral arrangements.

When recording the death, AIDS need not be entered on the death certificate since the primary cause of death is the opportunistic infection or cancer. Because death certificates are public documents the relatives or the patient may specifically request that AIDS is omitted to avoid stigmatisation. This does not affect the statistical records at the Centre for Communicable Disease Surveillance at Colindale since the death must be reported there separately and confidentially.

Post-mortem

Because AIDS is such a new disease, research is still needed to discover more about the disease process and treatment effects. Post-mortem examination can reveal vital information and is therefore usually requested. Relatives and friends generally recognise the research needs and usually give permission for this. They are also often keen to know the results. It is recommended by the

Department of Health that post-mortem examination of patients with AIDS must be undertaken only by a consultant pathologist with the assistance of experienced pathology technicians.

Care of the body

If the death occurs in hospital or a hospice last offices are performed as normal, and then the body is placed in a heavy duty plastic body bag. Nurses should wear disposable gloves and a plastic apron when performing last offices, but once the body is in the bag no further infection control precautions are required. However it is recommended that those handling the body, e.g. funeral personnel, should be informed of the potential risk of infection if there is contact with blood or body fluids. "Danger of Infection" labels on the body and body bag and accompanying paperwork may be used.

When the person dies at home the undertakers should be informed that there is an infection risk, although the diagnosis of AIDS does not need to be divulged. The undertakers will then bring a plastic body bag and place the body in it before removing it from the home.

Unless a post-mortem examination is to be performed, the body remains in the bag with no further attention until the funeral. Because embalming carries a risk of innoculation injury, this procedure is not carried out on bodies known to be infected with HIV.

For these reasons it is vital that those close to the patient are warned about the use of the body bag and that they are given adequate opportunity to say their goodbyes before the body is put in it. This applies both in hospital and at home. Any necessary religious rites should also be performed before the body goes into the bag. In some cultures it may need to be members of the family or of the same religion who place the body in the bag. This can cause difficulties in the hospital setting as it may delay the removal of the body to the mortuary.

Whenever possible it is best to discuss the care of the body with the next of kin before death occurs so that suitable arrangements can be made. It may even be appropriate to discuss this with the patient. Many patients plan their own funerals and have definite views about how they wish to be dressed after death.

Relatives, partners or other carers may wish to be involved in the laying out of the body. Laying out, or last offices, involves washing the deceased in a similar manner to a bed bath. Two people are needed to do this so that one can turn the body and lift limbs while the other is washing and drying. Hair is arranged and men are shaved. If there is leakage from any orifice, e.g., the rectum, cotton wool is packed into it using forceps or tweezers. However, this is not always necessary. The body is dressed in a shroud, or nightclothes, or according to the patient's or relative's wishes. The mouth can be kept closed until rigor mortis occurs by placing a pillow firmly under the jaw. False teeth are put in place before the jaw is closed.

District nurses in general do not carry out last offices when their patients die because the undertakers prepare the body in every way for the funeral. However, as this is not the case when someone with AIDS dies, district nurses need to be able to give the carers advice, or practical help with laying out at home. Funeral arrangements for cremation or burial can then be made in the usual way and in accordance with the patient's wishes.

Potential problems

Incidences of undertakers refusing to take someone who has died with AIDS have been reported and do still occur, but as the incidence of AIDS increases and spreads, this problem appears to be diminishing. It can be worthwhile to discuss this with the local funeral directors before a patient dies so that a suitable and sympathetic undertaker is known and the problem of rejection is averted.

In the case of gay men dying with AIDS there have been some incidences of conflict between the dead man's partner and his family over the management of the funeral, even to the exclusion of one or other party. This, of course, only adds stress to the bereavement and may prolong the grieving process. The Gay Bereavement Project or similar support groups can help in these circumstances.

Chapter 8

CARE OF THE BEREAVED

Grieving for a loved one begins long before that person dies. The needs of those close to the patient are as important as the patient's.

For the informal carers, i.e. the family, partner or friends, the task of caring may be unfamiliar and overwhelming. The stigma that is still associated with AIDS will prevent some from sharing their problems and needs with friends, relatives or other means of support. Relatives, especially parents, may be staying with the dying patient in order to provide care or to be close by. They are then separated from other family members and may be facing issues, like homosexuality and drug misuse, with which they are unfamiliar and uneasy. Others, like partners and friends, are often already grieving for people close to them who have died as a result of AIDS.

Isolation, for whichever reason, needs to be recognised and tackled by those providing care. Introduction to other people in a similar situation, or referral to a self-help group for families and friends of people with AIDS, can help. Professional and voluntary carers must also recognise their own roles in provid-ing support for informal carers, and allow sufficient time for listening, advising and encouragement. This needs to be approached sensitively so that the appropriate person or agency is available for support. For instance, some carers may not wish to be associated with self-help groups or individuals with a religious or a homosexual bias, while others may find these of particular benefit. In providing support, it should also be remembered that in many cases, whatever the route of HIV transmission, the informal carers are also infected with HIV and are viewing their own future whilst caring for a dying loved one. Guilt associated with the infection of the dying patient can overshadow the relationship between the patient and the carers.

At times the informal carers need respite from the burden of caring and they should be encouraged not to feel guilty about this need. Emphasis should be placed on the importance of maintaining their physical and mental health with adequate rest and relief from responsibilities so that they can continue to provide adequate care. Respite may be provided by admission of the patient to hospital or a hospice for a week or two, or by provision of statutory carers, e.g., home carers or community care assistants for a few hours every day, or a sitter at night. The dependent patient may also apply for an attendance allowance from the Department of Social Security to help pay for any extra care or other special needs.

As well as regular respite, informal carers need information and skills training to enable them to provide care. They need encouragement and appreciation, especially when the patient is not able to show this due to deteriorating mental or physical state. Most of all, informal carers need to be treated as partners by the professional carers, valued for their work and consulted about the services they receive. Information giving and consultation are vital aspects of the care of the bereaved. Although reactions to death vary widely according to previous experience, culture and personality, the fear of the unknown is almost universal. Before the patient dies explanation to the informal carers about the likely nature of the death need not be morbid but can help to prepare them. Similarly, clear instructions are needed, spoken and written, about what to do if the patient dies at home.

Being with the patient at the time of death is very important to most people. Those providing care should recognise this and try to ensure that relatives or friends not present are called in time. Some may need privacy at this time while others prefer the presence and support of professional carers. They should be given the choice.

After the death, some form of follow-up care for those left behind is vital. This needs to be the clear responsibility of one of the key workers, e.g., the social worker, the health advisor, HIV counsellor or community nurse.

For many bereaved the most difficult time is after the funeral. Mourning is an essential, natural process, for which many will receive adequate support from relatives and friends, but bereavement follow-up will identify those who need more formal help. Bereavement counselling will bring people through the process who would otherwise get inappropriately stuck at some stage in their grief.

For everyone, encouragement and appreciation from all sources needs to continue after the patient dies. Placing emphasis on the contribution made by the informal carers helps them to cope with the loss.

Similarly stressing the worth of the deceased can help in bereavement. This can take many forms. For instance it might be a speech at the funeral or memorial service, or something like a poem or an obituary written privately or for publication. In America many of the bereaved have made quilts in memory of those who have died with AIDS. Many people with AIDS have made major contributions to the care of other people with AIDS by working for voluntary organisations, raising funds or participating in research projects. Recognition of this, and other more general virtues attributable to the deceased, however small, need to be recognised and treasured by the bereaved.

Chapter 9

CARE FOR THE CARERS

The impact on professional carers of working with people with HIV and AIDS can be considerable. For all sorts of reasons health care workers and social services carers involved in the care of people dying with AIDS have particular need of support.

Most AIDS patients are relatively young, some very young, and caring for young dying people can be very distressing. It is easy for the health care workers and others to identify with the patients and the boundaries that normally exist between carer and client can become blurred. Some of the health care workers involved in the care of people with AIDS may have chosen a career, such as in genito-urinary medicine, which did not specifically involve care of the dying. They may feel ill-prepared to help young people face disfigurement, disability and death.

Personal and home issues may also intrude into the work situation. Negative attitudes towards caring for people with AIDS from spouse, lover or close friends, and the social stigma associated with AIDS may cause personal conflict. The multiple problems and needs of the patients can cause difficulty for workers in attempting to achieve a balance between time spent at home and at work.

It should be remembered that professional carers are bereaved when their clients/patients die and they need time to grieve. Whenever possible, staff who wish to, should be allowed time to attend the funeral, should be given help in saying their farewells, and in gaining a sense of completion of their care for the deceased. Some benefit may be gained from a post-mortem case conference when all those involved in the care get together to discuss what went well and what could have been done better. In this way everyone's contribution can be recognised, problems aired, and lessons learned for the care of future patients.

The care of people with AIDS is generally very rewarding, but the stresses involved in addition to other work-related stress can lead to 'burn-out'. This is a condition seen to arise in caring professionals when there is a discrepancy between the demands of the job and the ability of a member of staff to fulfill these demands for a variety of reasons. It is usually characterised by the member of staff becoming short-tempered, less able to do the job effectively and efficiently, unable to make decisions or to delegate work appropriately. Burn-out can occur in an individual member of staff, or may become apparent throughout a team. If the problem is not recognised and addressed, morale becomes low, absenteeism increases and a high turnover of staff follows.

It is therefore essential to take steps to prevent burn-out. In specialised settings, such as the hospice for people with AIDS or the HIV unit of care, formalised support groups for staff with professional facilitators (e.g. psychologists) are the most appropriate way to reduce stress. These should be arranged during work time and should be available to all disciplines and all grades at times to suit the various shifts.

In setting up support groups, certain decisions need to be made about how they are to function. The purpose of the group needs to be clear so that all those participating benefit and it doesn't become just another business meeting. The composition of the group, whether it is confined to one professional group or mixed, should be such that the members feel safe and comfortable to discuss their concerns.

Informal support between colleagues is also vital in all work settings. Whether this is in the work place or in a social environment depends upon the individuals involved. Listening to each other's day-to-day problems, sharing the workload and keeping good communication between the professionals all help

to reduce the risk of burn-out. Similarly, professional carers should recognise their responsibility to maintain their own health by having adequate rest from work and doing other activities unassociated with work.

To balance the stresses, there are the rewards of caring for people with AIDS. How carers get their rewards will be different for different individuals and groups. For those caring in the community it may be satisfying to be able to keep patients out of hospital. For hospital staff the rewards may come through changing practices to suit the individual patient's needs and wishes or through participating in research that leads to improved quality of life. Informal carers may get satisfaction from knowing that everything that could be done was done, and that they were able to do it. For all, the reward of facilitating a comfortable death is probably the greatest.

Further reading and reference

ABC of AIDS, Michael Adler, Ed., British Medical Journal publication, 1988.

AIDS, A Strategy for Nursing Care, Robert J. Pratt, Edward Arnold, 1986.

AIDS, Therapeutics in HIV Disease, Michael Youle, Janet Clarbour, Paul Wade and Charles Farthing. Churchill Livingstone, Edinburgh, 1988.

Caring for Someone with AIDS, Research Institute for Consumer Affairs, Consumers Association with Hodder & Stoughton, 1990.

"Classification System for Human Immunodeficiency Virus Infection in Children under 13 Years of Age", Centres for Disease Control in Morbidity & Mortality Weekly Report (April 24) 36:15: pp. 225-30, and 235-6 Atlanta, USA, 1987.

A Colour Atlas of AIDS and HIV Disease, Charles Farthing, Simon Brown, and Richard Staughton, Wolfe Medical Publications Ltd., 1988.

Goodbye, I Love You, C. L. Pearson, Pan Books, 1988.

A Guide to Clinical Counselling, Second Edition, Riva Miller and Robert Bor, Science Press, 1989.

Journal of Palliative Care, 1988, 4:4 (includes papers on out-patient treatment, diagnosis and management of pain in AIDS, and articles from hospices in different countries).

Living with AIDS: A Guide to Survival by People with AIDS, 1987, reprinted 1990, published by Frontliners and available from them. 9.95, but free to people with AIDS-Related Complex (ARC) or AIDS.

National AIDS Manual. This is a publication produced for organisations rather than individuals. It contains a comprehensive list of organisations and extensive information, and is updated regularly. It is available by subscription from NAM Publications Ltd., P.O. Box 99, London, SW2, Tel: 071 737 1846.

The Screaming Room, Barbara Peabody, Oak Tree Publications Inc., California, 1986.

Further Training for Nurses

The ENB 934 course in the "Care and Management of People with HIV Disease" is a short post-registration course covering the many issues involved in HIV disease. It is run in many centres across the country. Addresses available from the English National Board.

A distance learning package entitled AIDS: Meeting the Challenge, is published by the English National Board and is available in many colleges of nursing. Details from ENB Resource and Careers Services, Woodseats House, 764 Chesterfield Road, Sheffield S8 OSE.

Useful addresses

The following list is not comprehensive. Many national and local organisations provide a variety of general and specialist services. Details of these can be obtained from the National AIDS Helpline, the Terence Higgins Trust, and the National AIDS Manual noted above.

ACET (AIDS care education and training)
  PO Box 1323, London W5 5TF, Tel: 081 840 7879
  PO Box 108, Edinburgh EH8 9NY, Tel: 031 668 4225
  PO Box 153, Dundee DD1 9RH, Tel: 0382 202463
  PO Box 147, Portsmouth PO2 9DA, Tel: 0705 693422
A charity providing education and training, loans of equipment and grants for items such as furniture and telephone installation.

AIDS Helpline (Northern Ireland), PO Box 206, Belfast BT1 1FJ, Tel: 0232 326117. Provides information, counselling, and support (including a buddy service) and are associated with a Body Positive group.

Black HIV-AIDS Network (BHAN), BM MCC, London WC1 3XX, Tel: 071 792 1200 x 2156. A nationwide voluntary group for black and Asian people affected by HIV and AIDS, which offers counselling, community care and buddies, support groups, and education and training.

Blackliners, PO Box 74, London, SW12 9JY, Tel: 081 673 1695. Offers counselling about HIV, AIDS, and drug addiction to black and Asian people.

Body Positive, 51b Philbeach Gardens, London SW5 9EB, Tel: 071 373 9124. Body Positive was set up by people with HIV infection as a self-help group. There are now groups throughout the country which offer advice about HIV, practical help, support groups and information weekends. A newsletter is published each fortnight.

British Red Cross Society, 9 Grosvenor Crescent, London SW1X 7EJ, Tel: 071 235 5454. Provides local services which may benefit some patients with AIDS, including cosmetic camouflage, home nursing, and transport.

CRUSAID, 21A Upper Tachbrook Street, London SW1, Tel: 071 834 7566. AIDS fundraising charity providing money for community, public and individual needs.

CRUSE, Cruse House, 126 Sheen Road, Richmond, Surrey TW9 1UR, 081 940 4818. A national organisation offering support for the bereaved.

Frontliners UK Ltd., The Frontliners' Centre, 55 Farringdon Road, London, EC1M 3JB, Tel: 071 430 1199. Frontliners Scottish Division, 37-39 Montrose Terrace, Edinburgh EH7 5DJ, Tel: 031 652 0754. Frontliners is a registered charity set up and run by people with AIDS or ARC to provide education and emotional, practical, and financial support throughout the country. They also publish a regular newsletter.

Gay Bereavement Project, Unitarian Rooms, Hoop Lane, London NW11, Tel: 081 455 8894. A charity offering support and counselling by telephone. They also advise on making wills, and have produced a simple will form for use if everything is to be left to a partner.

The Haemophilia Society, 123 Westminster Bridge Road, London SE1 7HR, Tel: 071 928 2020.

Health Literature Line, PO Box 1577, London NW1 3DW, Tel: 0800 555777. Send free leaflets and books about HIV and AIDS.

Lantern Trust, 72 Honey Lane, Waltham Abbey, Essex EN9 3BS, Tel: 0992 714900. Provides publications and training courses for health care professionals working with people with HIV.

London Lighthouse, 111/117 Lancaster Road, London W11 1OT, Tel: 071 792 1200. Provides information and training courses, counselling, support groups, and a drop-in centre and cafe, as well as the residential unit and home support service.

Macmillan nurses - information available from: Cancer Relief (Macmillan Fund), Anchor House, 15-19 Britten Street, London, SW3 3TY, Tel: 071 351 7811. Macmillan teams were originally set up to help people with cancer by providing home support and assistance with pain and symptom control. In some Health Districts they are also able to help people with any incurable disease, including AIDS.

Mainliners, PO Box 125, London SW9 8EF, Tel: 071 274 4000 Ext. 354. A Charity providing information and support for drug users and former drug users affected by HIV infection, and their friends and families.

Marie Curie Cancer Care, Community Nursing Department, 28 Belgrave Square, London SW1X 8Q6, Tel: 071 235 3325

Marie Curie Cancer Care, 21 Rutland Street, Edinburgh EH1 2AH, Tel: 031 229 8332. The Marie Curie Community Nursing Service gives practical home nursing support to people with cancer, and can also help people with AIDS and cancer

Mildmay Mission Hospital, Hackney Road, London E2 7NA, Tel: 071 739 2331. Provides a hospice unit, day centre, and home care team for people with AIDS, and training courses for health care workers.

National AIDS Helpline, Tel: 0800 567 123. Free helpline providing up-to-date information about services related to HIV.

Positively Women, 333 Gray's Inn Road, London WC1X 8PX, 071 837 9705. A self-help group for women with HIV.

Scottish AIDS Monitor (SAM), National Office, PO Box 48, Edinburgh EH1 5SA Tel: 031 557 3885. Glasgow Office, PO Box 111, Glasgow G2 2UT, Tel: 041 204 1127. Provides information, counselling, support (including a buddy scheme), and advice on welfare rights to people in Scotland.

Terence Higgins Trust, 52-54 Gray's Inn Road, London WC1X 8LT, Tel: 071 831 0330, Helpline: 071 242 1010 (3 pm - 10 pm) The major national organisation for information and support required in relation to HIV infection. It provides advice on welfare and legal issues, counselling, support groups, a range of publications and access (by appointment) to a comprehensive library.

Turning Point, 9-12 Long Lane, London, EC1A 9HA, National network of support centres for drug users and their friends and relatives.

The Lisa Sainsbury Foundation Series

Vera Darling and Prue Clench, Editors, Austen Cornish Publishers Ltd. in association with the Lisa Sainsbury Foundation. All books are available in paperback only, and directly from the Lisa Sainsbury Foundation, 8-10 Crown Hill, Croydon CR0 1RY.

Caring for Dying People of Different Faiths, Julia Neuberger

Missed Beginnings: death before life has been established, June Jolly

Pain Control, Jane Latham

Communicating with Dying People and their Relatives, Jean Lugton

Radiotherapy, Susan Holmes

Loss and Bereavement, Bridget Cook and Shelagh Phillips

Cancer Chemotherapy, Susan Holmes (in press)